TRUSTLANDS

Swan Pond, Culzean Castle Country Park.

TRUSTLANDS

PHOTOGRAPHS OF THE NATIONAL TRUST FOR SCOTLAND
BY GLYN SATTERLEY

INTRODUCED BY MAGNUS MAGNUSSON

Published in association with

🜲 National Trust for Scotland

Chambers

Published by W & R Chambers Ltd, Edinburgh,
1989

**British Library Cataloguing in Publication
Data**
  Satterley, Glyn
  Trustlands: photographs of the National Trust
  for Scotland.
  1. Scotland. Buildings of historical importance.
  Organisations: National Trust for Scotland
  I. Title
  363.6'9'060411

ISBN 0-550-21006-7

Photography on Kodak film

Design by Patricia Macdonald

Colour origination by Bordercolour, Brampton,
Cumbria

Typeset by Waddie & Co. Ltd., Edinburgh

Printed in Great Britain by The Eagle Press PLC

CONTENTS

ACKNOWLEDGEMENTS

I am indebted to so many people who helped (albeit some of them unknowingly) create this book that I would like to take this chance to try and thank them all. I am particularly grateful to Micky Blacklock of the National Trust for Scotland, who by his enthusiasm for the project, and subsequent gaining of the necessary funding made this book possible. Also to the Trust staff in Edinburgh, especially those in the Stockbridge Studio and in particular Sue Anderson, Jim Proudfoot, John Forgie, Judy Aitken, Ian Boyter and Vivien Bremner. All helped me tremendously, in spite of being continuously asked to rack their brains to answer my barrage of questions about various properties and activities.

Thank you too, to the numerous on-site representatives, rangers, gardeners and administrators of the Trust who were so generous with their time and expertise; especially Alan Whitfield of Kintail, Lea MacNally of Torridon, Willie Elliot of Glencoe, David Mardon of Ben Lawers, Kevin Rideout of St Abb's, Bill Hean of Threave, Derrick Warner of Brodick, Stewart Thomson of Fair Isle, Chrissie McGillivray of Burg, The MacKinnon family of Canna, Gordon Riddle of Culzean, Rhona Moir of Culloden and Philip Schreiber of the West Region office, Glasgow.

Special thanks are due to Kodak, who sponsored the photography and to Caledonian MacBrayne, who helped me get around the West Coast Islands.

Last, but not least, I would like to thank the following: Pat Macdonald for her excellent, sensitive design work (and thank you for not cropping my pictures), Alastair Fyfe Holmes of Chambers for his patience and encouraging response to the idea from the outset, and a huge thanks to Andrea my wife, for steering me through it all, editing, correcting and, fortunately for me, being able to share a few of the trips.

PREFACE

Over the last few years I have become increasingly aware that the National Trust for Scotland is not only a preserver of battle sites and ancient castles, but also guardian of some of the wildest and most spectacular landscapes in Europe.

It was my interest in the tremendous scale and variety of these areas, as well as the people who work, live on and maintain them, which inspired this book. Particularly places like Fair Isle and Canna, where entire communities were inherited. The project was made possible by the generous sponsorship of Kodak, and by the support of the Trust who allowed me a free hand to concentrate on whichever aspects interested me. These photographs are therefore a personal look at the Trustlands taken periodically over two years.

The project has involved the organisation of many trips and thousands of miles covered by car, boat, plane and on foot. Needless to say there were hiccups – such as watching all my equipment drop from a great height into a waterfall at Kintail (fortunately saved and dried out harmlessly); or being stranded on St Kilda with my clothing, provisions and the bulk of my film on the boat heading back to Oban, thanks to worsening weather conditions; plus a few bouts of sea-sickness I would rather forget! Nevertheless the project has been one of the most enjoyable I have ever undertaken.

Memories range from a wonderful sunny week on Fair Isle amongst the islanders, haymaking, clipping, fishing and bringing home the peats, to five damp days on St Kilda when cloud barely left ground level; from a blustery Autumn hike out to the fossil tree at the Burg, to my surprise and delight in discovering Edinburgh's Caiy Stone stranded in the middle of a housing estate and the beautiful Loch Skeen hidden away as it is above the Grey Mare's Tail in the Borders.

With such a wealth of places to explore, I could never hope to do them all justice. The book, however, was never intended to be a comprehensive guide to the National Trust for Scotland, but rather a glimpse into its character and colour as I experienced it, in the hope that it might tempt others to go out and explore the Trustlands.

G.S.   March 1989

**Ferns outside the Parterre garden wall,
Pitmedden.**

INTRODUCTION

by Magnus Magnusson

This book is a celebration of the National Trust for Scotland and all that it stands for. It is neither a formal guide nor a gazetteer, but an affectionate pictorial exploration of the nature of the Trust and what one might call the 'Trustlands'. It is not the Trust's view of itself, nor even the popular view of the Trust: many people, I suspect, think of the Trust as being only 'about' old buildings and historic furnishings, castles and manicured gardens — a massive self-indulgent exercise in national nostalgia. This book of photographs is an alternative view of the Trust: it is a cool outsider's view, a one-man view — and not even a Scottish view, at that. But perhaps because the eye of the beholder is looking from the outside, it sees right to the core.

Glyn Satterley is as English as they come. He is a Kentishman from Sevenoaks with an uncompromisingly southern accent. But he had worked in Scotland as a telephone engineer before he studied painting at Art College at Ravensbourne near Bromley; there he moved into photography, and came back to Scotland as a photographer to do a project in Caithness and Sutherland. He married a Scots girl, and has now been living in Edinburgh for the past ten years.

He has always been interested in Scottish landscape, and has done occasional work on specific aspects of the Trust. He found himself fascinated by the immense variety of the environments ('about ten times greater than that of the English National Trust') and he wanted to try to cover this great diversity in a book; and in so doing, to incorporate a great deal more — the people who work for the Trust, and the people whom the Trust has inherited, so to speak, and the kind of activities that go on within those environments. The scope is therefore much broader than just a book of handsome landscapes.

In fact it was while he was working on a commission for the Trust on Fair Isle, the most isolated inhabited island in Britain, that the idea for the book began to germinate. He was as much entranced with the island community life (which the Trust has done so much to stimulate) as with the Bird Observatory that has made it world famous.

To achieve the superb pictures in this book, he walked for miles with deer-stalkers and Rangers over hill and moor. He got himself marooned for several days on St Kilda, he went to sea with the crab-fishermen off St Abb's Head, he even dropped his camera equipment into a waterfall!

What I find particularly refreshing about this book, quite apart from the skill and artistry of the camera-work, is the way in which Glyn Satterley has presented the people of the Trust. Here we meet quintessential countrymen like Stewart Thomson, the Trust representative on Fair Isle, and Willie Elliot, the Ranger/Naturalist of Glencoe, and Lea MacNally of Torridon, himself an author and outstanding photographer in his own right; a former army colonel, Bill Cockburn, at Brodie Castle, who is the very epitome of a Trust representative, ready to turn his hand to whatsoever needs doing; a former Loganair pilot, Alan Whitfield, who is now the Resident Representative and Ranger for

Kintail and Morvich; great experts in their own right, like John Basford, the head gardener at Brodick Castle, who is a world authority on rhododendrons; great craftsmen with age-old skills, like heather-thatcher Jeremy Cox from Castle Douglas working on the roof of Old Leanach Cottage at Culloden; the veteran gardener at Inverewe, Billy Mackenzie, who came with the garden when the Trust inherited it in 1952; and the granny of them all, crofter Chrissie McGillivray of The Burg on Mull, at over 90 years of age the Trust's oldest employee, and in charge of the Trust's oldest property — the 50-million-year-old Fossil Tree (it was also one of the very first properties to come into the Trust's care, by bequest in 1932).

How pleasing it is to meet them all in these pages; for one of the most endearing aspects of the National Trust for Scotland is the way in which its representatives become so intimately attached to 'their' properties. The Trust has been described as Scotland's strangest landlord; but I always think of it as the Nation's Caretaker, in the noblest sense of that term. The men and women who work for it care passionately for the nation and its heritage; for them, the work is more than just a job, it is a calling. They have given the very word 'Trust' new dimension; it is so much more than just a legalistic term of statutory obligation. They identify wholeheartedly with the places in their care. They tend to say, 'When I inherited the property', as if it were a personal family possession; and that is to all intents and purposes what it is, except that in their case the family is the whole nation. They see their job as a vocation, and they are always trying to enhance their property, in order to hand it on to posterity in even better shape than when they came to it.

No property is ever allowed to stagnate and become merely a wilderness or a mausoleum of the past; conservation and restoration are a continuing dynamic. They are endlessly curious, always trying to find out more about the property in order to share their new knowledge with their visitors. I'm sure there are still fascinating discoveries to be made at every one of the Trust's historic properties. Take Brodick Castle on the Island of Arran, for instance, the ancient seat of the Dukes of Hamilton and one of the oldest habitable houses owned by the Trust; one might have thought that there was nothing more to do about it. The magnificent sandstone castle has survived the most extraordinary vicissitudes of history. It is set in 65 acres of spectacular gardens; behind it lie 7,300 acres of mountain, hill and moor that form a perfect microcosm of Scotland's majestic topography. But the work of restoration, both inside and out, never stops; and, as recently as 1980, a Bronze Age cist burial containing a decorated food vessel was unearthed in the Old Deer Park in the Castle demesnes, to add to the island's astonishing wealth of ancient monuments from prehistoric times.

Or take Fyvie Castle in Buchan, with its five towers enshrining five centuries of turbulent Scottish history. This is the latest of the castles to be acquired by the Trust, in 1984 (with generous help from the National Heritage Memorial Fund). With its superb collection of portraits by artists like Raeburn, Ramsay, Gainsborough and Opie, it is perhaps the most opulent example of baronial architecture in Scotland, complete with landscaped parkland and a man-made loch. But Fyvie also has a 'secret room' below the Charter Room, which has never been opened, because to do so would operate an otherwise latent curse whose traditional effect is the death of the laird and the blindness of his wife. Now that the lairdship of Fyvie has changed so radically, I will be surprised, to say the least, if some Trust representative doesn't have a go sometime in the future!

Nor is it only a question of new and spectacular discoveries. Many Trust properties are crammed with material that awaits fresh interpretation for the public. At Leith Hall in Grampian, which was the seat of the martial Leith family for more than three centuries, the magnificent collection of military memorabilia has now been put on display in five rooms on the top floor of the east wing in an exhibition entitled 'For Crown and Country – the Military Lairds of Leith Hall'.

This book reflects the enormous diversity of the Trust's interests, a matchless universe of contrasts, from the desolate wildness of St Kilda to the almost comic urbanity of one of the very smallest of the Trust properties – the so-called Caiy Stone, on the north side of Oxgangs Road, Edinburgh. (I had always thought it to be the smallest, but that distinction evidently goes to the granite Bruce's Stone on Moss Raploch in the Stewartry of Dumfries & Galloway, marking the spot where Robert the Bruce defeated the English in 1307). It's a bizarre monument to find in a city, a handsome, 9-ft-tall sandstone monolith commemorating some long-forgotten battle and now standing nonchalantly on the pavement as if waiting for the Fairmilehead bus!

What an extraordinary contrast it makes to St Kilda, the island archipelago that died when its tiny community was evacuated in 1930 – only to find new life in 1957 when it was bequeathed to the Trust and then leased as a National Nature Reserve to the Nature Conservancy Council (which then sub-leased a portion of the main island of Hirta to the Ministry of Defence as a missile-tracking station). St Kilda was always the farthest habitable frontier, the last lonely bastion of the west. Those magnificent sea-cliffs (the highest in the British Isles) rearing abruptly out of the heaving Atlantic, those strange beehive cells or 'cleits' that served as larder and storehouse combined for the villagers of Hirta, those indigenous goat-like sheep named after the nearby island of Soay – little wonder that St Kilda was designated by UNESCO in 1987 as Scotland's first World Heritage Site.

The Trust is now landlord to 101 properties, covering 100,000 acres and scattered all over Scotland from St Abb's Head in Berwickshire out to St Kilda, and from the Solway Firth up to Fair Isle. The 100th property to come on the books, as it were, was the romantic, uninhabited island of Staffa, off Iona, with its renowned Fingal's Cave and glorious basalt formations. It came into the Trust's

care in 1986 in fairy-tale fashion: the President of the Scottish National Trust Golden Jubilee Foundation (USA), Mr John Elliott, Jr, of New York, who is the Chairman Emeritus of Ogilvy and Mather, gave it to the Trust as an imaginative way of honouring his wife's birthday – and she was declared Steward of Staffa for her lifetime in recognition of this munificent gift. Property No 101 was the marvellous vintage printing works at Innerleithen in the Borders, Robert Smail's Printing Works, which the Trust is planning to re-open as a working printing museum.

Today the National Trust for Scotland has a large and rapidly growing membership of more than 179,000, with an income of about £8 million a year (including various grants). It welcomes some 1.7 million visitors annually to those of its properties where a count is maintained – but the actual figure must be at least double that, if you include those who visit its countryside properties and open areas. Every year the army of Trust enthusiasts grows. And every year, too, the Trust attractions grow, with new features and facilities for visitors to enjoy at its properties.

At the National Nature Reserve at St Abb's Head, north of Coldingham in Berwickshire, where the Northumbrian princess Æbbe founded a monastery in the 7th century AD, there is a new Nature Reserve Centre in a traditional steading at Northfield Farm which features the teeming bird-life that finds sanctuary on its spectacular 300-ft cliffs. St Abb's is not just the most important nesting colony for seabirds in south-eastern Scotland but also a significant staging-post on bird migration routes – a veritable Crewe Junction of the avian flight-paths. In addition, the inshore waters form part of Scotland's first voluntary marine nature reserve.

New interpretative work is always going on. In the enchanting little Royal Burgh of Culross on the north shore of the Forth, I myself had the privilege last year of opening a new Visitor Centre in the magnificent old Town House, which has been the beating heart of civic life in the burgh ever since it was built in 1626. When

the Town Council was abolished during local govern-
ment reorganisation, it handed the Town House
over to the Trust, which has now given it a renewed
lease of life. Culross is one of the proudest flagships of
the Trust and all that it stands for: a marvellously
preserved exemplar of a Scottish burgh of the 16th and
17th centuries, a living tapestry of the social history of
the Scottish industrial and trade renaissance in the reign
of James VI. For more than 50 years the Trust has
patiently and lovingly secured the conservation and
refurbishment of more and more of its Little Houses.
But Culross is more than just a showpiece; it is a three-
dimensional piece of history whose solid stone fabric
speaks the past more eloquently than any written
document could ever do.

At Falkland, which also has its Little Houses and the
magnificent Palace with its gardens and parkland that was
once the country retreat of the romantic and doom-laden
Stewart kings and queens, the Trust has recently bought
Falkland Town Hall. It will be opening in 1989 complete
with a new exhibition on 'The Royal Burgh', along with
suitable educational facilities. It adds yet another
dimension to the experience of the Royal Palace, which is
still the property of the sovereign and therefore must be
classed as the principal historic building in the Trust's
great estate.

At Culloden, scene of the last battle to be fought on
mainland Britain, in 1746, the battlefield has been cleared
of trees and re-seeded and restored to its original
moorland state. It is much easier now to recreate in the
mind's eye the harrowing agony with which the final
Jacobite rising came to its inevitable, sorrowing end, and
to understand much more clearly how and why it
happened. The excellent Visitor Centre with its colourful
historical displays is constantly being improved and
refined; and Old Leanach Cottage (the only building in
the area to have survived the battle), which used to serve
as the Visitor Centre, has been re-equipped with period
furnishings and a life-size model of a grieving young
mother and baby.

There are new interpretative displays at the Rotunda at
Bannockburn, in the shadow of the magnificent
equestrian statue of Robert the Bruce, by Pilkington
Jackson. They happily reinforce the new 'Kingdom of the
Scots' exhibition in the Centre itself. Ah, Bannockburn!
The very name is like a tocsin. And that magic date, June
1314, when the Bruce defeated the armed might of
Edward II and laid the foundations for an independent
nation — that is part of the litany that every Scottish
schoolchild knows.

This book is about the heartlands of the Trust, of the
central Trust experience, indeed of nature and identity of
Scotland itself. It is the encapsulation of what Scotland is
in all its glorious variety, the great and small, the old and
the new, the natural and the man-made. Like the
Tenement House in Glasgow, they are not all large
historic houses or picturesque cottages; they didn't all
belong to princes or prelates. Like the bizarre structure
known as The Pineapple at Airth, near the Kincardine
Bridge, which was built as a retreat in 1761, they are not
all exemplary models of baronial architecture — the
Pineapple has now been restored as a self-catering
holiday home for ordinary people. The picturesque folly
of The Hermitage near Dunkeld is not a perfectly
sculpted granite statement such as Crathes Castle on
Deeside, more of a quaint footnote. The sombre peaks of
Glencoe, scene of the 1692 massacre of the Macdonalds
by the Campbells, or the ancient oakwoods of the Forest
of Drum, are far removed from the formalised serenity of
the beautiful Great Garden of Pitmedden in Grampian.

It is now more than a dozen years since I had the
honour of contributing the General Introduction to *The
National Trust for Scotland Guide* in 1976. It is almost a
decade since I wrote my own book on some of the
Trust's castles and great houses, entitled *Treasures of
Scotland* in 1981. Since then there have been numerous
other publications, both specialised and general, about the
Trust and all its works. Yet the final word is never
spoken; the Trust is too dynamic an organisation for
anyone ever to have the last word. The Trust is not so

much a corporation as a cause, a crusade, a culture in its own right. Glyn Satterley's vision of the Trust, as realised in this splendid portfolio, goes beyond the word; it gives us a glancing and penetrating view — dancing glints and gleaming glimpses of the great wealth of human and heritage resources that the Trust husbands on behalf of us all.

M.M.   March 1989

Early morning lambing round, Canna.

THE PHOTOGRAPHS

Fair Isle
Shetland

**Overlooking the main township of
Fair Isle, from Malcolm's Head.**

**Stewart Thomson, the Trust's
representative on Fair Isle.**
As well as carrying out his Trust duties,
Stewart runs a croft, manages the airport,
fixes all things mechanical, and plays a mean
fiddle. He is warmly respected as the island
community leader.

Haymaking in August.

Taking the peats home, August.
The peats are cut in early summer, stacked
for air-drying, and restacked a couple of
times during the summer, before they are
finally ready to take home.

A summertime barbecue on the beach at North Haven.
The music-makers span three generations of Thomsons — Stewart Snr, Stewart Jnr, and his son Ewan.

West Coast, evening.

Inverewe
Ross and Cromarty,
Highland

**Billy Mackenzie, Gardener, Inverewe
Gardens.**
Billy has cared for the plants at Inverewe
since before the Trust took the Gardens over
in 1952.

The Large Pond.

Towards Poolewe, overlooking azaleas.
The Gardens at the end of May are superb, emphasising their contrast with the infertile environment of Inverewe.

Rhododendron Walk (*left*).

Inverewe variety, late May (*right*).
A representation of such a wide range of plants and trees, on such a northern latitude, is unique to Inverewe.

Torridon
Ross and Cromarty, Highland

Overlooking Loch Torridon, from above Inveralligin.

**Walker passing the west slopes of
Beinn Eighe.**

A family of walkers, the west slopes of Beinn Eighe.

Stranded rowan on slopes of Liathach.

Lichen detail, Liathach.

Kite-flying on Loch Torridon shore,
Liathach behind.

Lea MacNally with two-day-old red deer calf.
Lea has been the ranger at Torridon for 20 years. Originally a professional deerstalker, he is a highly respected naturalist, writer and wildlife photographer, considered to be one of the leading authorities on red deer and golden eagles.

Inspecting an eagle's eyrie.
In June, Lea and I made a climb up to the site of an eagle's nest hoping it might be occupied. Unfortunately, we found no eagle, but to watch Lea in that mountain-top environment, hopping around like a schoolboy on a tree branch, was well worth the effort.

Culloden
Inverness,
Highland

Re-thatching Old Leanach Cottage.

Thatcher and visitors, Old Leanach Cottage.
When necessity arises, the Trust employs various specialist craftsmen. The Old Cottage at Culloden, which has stood there since before the battle of 1746, needed a new roof. So Jem Cox, a thatcher from Castle Douglas, was brought in and re-thatched it in local heather.

Cloud and Hanoverian Army flag.

Photographer and Jacobite flags.
Up until 1981 the actual battlefield had been
forested by trees. Since then the Trust has
purchased the ground, cleared the trees,
diverted a main road, and is stimulating a
natural regeneration of the land.

Clava Cairns
Inverness,
Highland

Clava Cairns and Standing Stones.
Clava is a place of great tranquillity. Normally
overshadowed by its notorious neighbour
Culloden, visually I found it far more
inspiring.

Standing Stone, Clava Cairns.

Brodie Castle
Moray,
Grampian

Brodie of Brodie.
Ninian, the 25th Brodie of Brodie, still lives
in the castle and frequently delights visitors
by giving them a personal tour of his family
home.

Window-cleaning, Brodie Castle.
Trust representative Bill Cockburn, an
ex-army Colonel, has to tackle more than the
paperwork at Brodie.

Kintail
Skye and Lochalsh,
Highland

**Walking the dog, by the shore of Loch
Duich.**
The Five Sisters of Kintail as a backdrop.
February, and the only real winter weather
I was able to experience.

Stalking ponies wintering in Glen Shiel.

Alan Whitfield, the Trust ranger, and Max, looking at the back of the Five Sisters, from the Ben Attow ridge. A day walking on Kintail ridges getting sunburned in shirtsleeves.

Deerstalking

Deerstalking is carried out on the Torridon, Kintail and Glencoe properties of the Trust, as a form of deer management, but never for sporting purposes. It is necessary in order to limit numbers of red deer to a thriving level in the hills. Just as a field can feed a certain number of sheep or cattle, a hill area can support only a certain number of deer. Maintaining this optimum number of deer on the hill grazing available, particularly during the long Highland winter, is the essence of red deer management. Culling the old and sick animals achieves this, in the way natural predators, like wolf and lynx, would have done.

Spying for stags.
The carrying ponies, hired for the duration of the season, were grateful for a break from the steep track heading towards Creag Ghlas. The party had set off earlier, with the aim of culling two stags – wind and weather permitting.

One stalk complete.
The dead stag is dragged down from where it was shot to a more suitable place for being loaded on to the awaiting pony.

Homeward bound.
Two stags successfully culled, but not without the whole party getting absolutely soaked in the process, owing to constant October showers.

**The River Croe, Gleann Lichd, with
Meall a' Charra in the distance.**

Pitmedden
Gordon,
Grampian

Parterre, Pitmedden Garden.

Ian Ross, Head Gardener, Pitmedden.

33

Drum
Kincardine and Deeside,
Grampian

The Old Forest of Drum.

Bracken-clearers in the Old Forest of Drum.
A team of pigs have been located in the forest, to determine their bracken-clearing potential. Other methods have proved unsuccessful, and the forest floor has become so densely covered with bracken that it is hindering the natural regeneration of plants and trees.

Leith Hall
Gordon,
Grampian

**View from the official viewpoint,
Hilltop, Leith Hall.**
Most of the Trust's great houses in the
Grampian area are set amidst superb
countryside. However, seeing this in relation
to the house is always a problem, largely
because of shelter belts of trees protecting
the houses and obscuring the view.

Fyvie Castle
Banff and Buchan,
Grampian

Fyvie Castle with frost.

Fyvie Loch, autumn.

Castle Fraser
Gordon,
Grampian

Castle Fraser.

Craigievar Castle
Gordon,
Grampian

The Castle cat and observer.

Crathes Castle
Kincardine and Deeside,
Grampian

Annual August topiary-cutting.

Herbaceous border.

Killiecrankie
Perth and Kinross,
Tayside

Riverside walk, early autumn.

Linn of Tummel
Perth and Kinross,
Tayside

The Garry Bridge, autumn.

The Garry Bridge, spring.

The Hermitage
Perth and Kinross,
Tayside

The Hermitage.
Originally the folly was more elaborate, and
at one time the inside walls and ceiling were
covered in mirrors to enhance the
atmosphere from the river below. It was here
that Wordsworth had an inspirational
'Moment of time'. Recently it has been
refurbished, an experience not new to it since
it was first vandalised in 1821 and then
blown up in 1869!

Branklyn Garden
Perth and Kinross,
Tayside

**Japanese Maple, Branklyn Garden,
Perth.**

Ben Lawers
Perth and Kinross, Tayside

Photographing mountain flowers, Ben Lawers.

Ben Lawers is a unique environment. Here flowers and plants, usually associated with areas of much higher altitudes such as the Alps or even the Himalayas, thrive. David Mardon, the ranger, has the task of organising the conservation of this plant-life and the mountain environment in general, which is under constant threat by increasing numbers of visitors. To help make people more aware of the habitat, David has perfected his own technique of producing superb magnified photographs of the Ben Lawers flora, many of which are minute and, seen life-size, seem quite insignificant.

Alpine gentian, Gentiana nivalis, July.
This is one of David Mardon's close-up photographs. This example is approximately 13mm high life-size.

A black lochan, Ben Lawers.

The Pineapple
Stirling,
Central

The Pineapple.
Incongruously poised like an ad-man's paste-up, this bizarre garden retreat is now let as a holiday home.

Hill of Tarvit
Fife

From the toposcope, Hill of Tarvit, looking west.

Kellie Castle
Fife

Kellie Castle Garden.

Balmerino Abbey
Fife

Crutched Spanish chestnut tree, Balmerino Abbey.
Refreshing to see that this old tree has been given an extra lease of life through the support of some of its sagging limbs.

Falkland Palace
Fife

Orchard produce, Falkland Palace.

Culross
Fife

Skateboarding, Tan House Brae, Culross.
For much of the time exploring 16th and 17th century Culross felt like walking round an empty film set. Occasionally though I glimpsed figures such as the lads on the skateboard, who seemed to sum up the juxtaposition of old and new, particularly with Grangemouth in the background.

Dysart
Fife

Dysart, Kirkcaldy.
A group of beautifully restored 'little houses' on the banks of the Forth.

Caiy Stone
Edinburgh,
Lothian

The Caiy Stone.
One of the biggest surprises, particularly as
I am a resident of Edinburgh, was finding
this small property, off Oxgangs Road,
surrounded by a housing estate.

Preston Mill
East Lothian,
Lothian

**The goose patrol, Preston Mill,
East Linton.**

St Abb's Head Nature Reserve
Berwickshire, Borders

St Abb's Head.

Crab fishermen, off St Abb's Head Nature Reserve.

Clifftops, St Abb's Head Nature Reserve.

The 'basement', St Abb's Head Nature Reserve.

Priorwood Garden
Ettrick and Lauderdale,
Borders

**Dried-flower arrangers, Priorwood
Garden, Melrose.**
This is the centre of the dried-flower
business at Priorwood. Tucked away in a
corner of the garden, from the outside it is a
small wooden hut – inside, an Aladdin's cave.

Flowers for drying.

Loch Skeen
Annandale and Eskdale,
Dumfries and Galloway

Loch Skeen.
A beautiful loch, hidden away above the Grey
Mare's Tail waterfall. Unfortunately the
clammy conditions I experienced had
encouraged the midge population out for an
evening sortie.

St Kilda
Western Isles

Welcome to St Kilda.
A message to the occasional important visitors who arrive by air; usually mainland visitors have the ordeal of 24 hours in a boat from Oban. My welcome was being stranded there because of worsening weather conditions, with clothing, provisions and the bulk of my film still on the boat heading back to Oban. Luckily the warden, David Miller, allowed me and two fellow travellers to stay in one of the renovated Village Bay houses and supplied us with ample food. I was disappointed that weather seldom improved during the five days I was there, though for St Kilda I suppose it was normal.

East coast cliffs, Hirta.
These sea-cliffs carry the distinction of being
the highest in the British Isles.

**Soay sheep, Hirta, with Stack Levenish
in the distance.**
Rarely on the island are you on level ground,
and I well believe reports that St Kildans
evolved strong ankles and broad feet to cope
with this; these also helped them climb the
sea stacks when gathering birds and eggs.

Rooftop grazing, Village Bay, Hirta.

Organic cleit, Hirta.

Cleits and enclosures, Hirta.
Cleits were used by the St Kildans for storage and air-drying food such as sea birds, eggs and fish. They are everywhere on Hirta, spanning the hillsides like rows of ancient grouse butts. These large enclosures would have been used for holding sheep, but there are some smaller, more circular, ones within the village which were used for sheltered cultivation of vegetables.

Iona
Argyll,
Strathclyde

Massey Ferguson, crofter and dog.
Since 1979 the Trust has owned Iona, with
the exception of the Abbey, a few other
buildings and historic sites. As with its other
inhabited island properties, it is responsible as
landlord for the human community as well as
the habitat.

Sheep tracks, west coast, 23.3.88.

Fionnphort jetty, 24.3.88.
This morning a force 9 gale meant that the
Iona ferry was cancelled, unbelievable after
the summerlike calm of the previous day.

Burg
Argyll,
Strathclyde

Burg headland, from Gowan Brae, Mull.

Chrissie McGillivray, Burg Farm, Mull.
Chrissie is the last of four generations of her family to live at Burg. Since 1936, when the Trust took over the property, she has been guardian of this superb area, actually known as 'The Wilderness', and has become a character much loved by visitors from far and wide. After my exhausting hike out to the 50-million-year-old fossil tree, she greeted me, in her usual style, with a very welcome cup of tea and a jam scone.

Fossil tree walkway, Burg, Mull.
The final section of the track out to
MacCulloch's fossil tree can only be
negotiated when the tide is out, and even
then the boulder-strewn promontory makes
it far from easy to reach the tree. The actual
remains of the tree were a disappointment to
me — visually overshadowed by the
impressive basalt forms to its right.

Staffa
Argyll,
Strathclyde

**Lobster fisherman with buoy,
Fingal's Cave.**
The waters around Staffa and its
neighbouring islands, as well as being a
resource for summer visitors, are very much
a place of work for others all year round.

Tourist boat in basalt landscape.

Basalt columns, east side.

Basalt columns, west side.

Visitor and basalt columns, east side.

Puffin.

I spent a whole day on Staffa, from early morning to evening, most of the time trying to come to terms with the basalt columns which I found intriguing. It was the puffins, however, that brought home the magic of the place for me, performing their clumsy aerobatics as I ate my lunch.

Canna
Lochaber,
Highland

Afternoon Stroll.

The Mackinnon family have been resident on Canna since about 1600. Today, father Ian manages the estate farm, helped by sons Dan and Patrick. Daughter Winefride, seen here walking with her husband and dog, assists father in his other role as Trust representative.

Springtime ploughing.
If anyone asked me to describe my idea of an
idyllic west coast island, it would be Canna.
In the main a working, farming community,
and unlike those on many west coast islands,
it survives without any real concessions to
tourism.

Dog and Sanday Church.

Shepherding (*left*).

Dan Mackinnon with separated lamb (*opposite*).
I followed Dan around for the best part of four days, dawn until dusk, determined to catch him lambing one of his ewes amidst the wonderful Canna landscape. In due course Dan obliged, several times, but inevitably behind walls or in corners of fields.

Feeding the ewes at lambing time.

Glenfinnan
Lochaber,
Highland

**Before the dancing commences,
Glenfinnan Games.**

Judging the piping, Glenfinnan Games.

Glencoe
Lochaber,
Highland

Glencoe, evening.

Willie Elliot, ranger, Glencoe.
As well as taking people to the hills on
guided walks throughout the summer, Willie
spends a lot of his time, particularly in winter,
assisting with mountain rescues. One of the
few residents in the Glen, he has lived all his
life in the cottage by Loch Achtriochtan.

Hilltop Walk, Aonach Eagach ridge.

Buachaille Etive Beag, winter.

Lomond
Strathclyde

Bucinch Island, Loch Lomond.
The Trust, which acquired Ben Lomond in 1984, has owned two uninhabited islands in Loch Lomond, Bucinch and Ceardach, since 1943.

Brewing tea, summit of Ben Lomond.

The Hill House
Helensburgh,
Strathclyde

**Cleaning the bedroom, The Hill
House.**

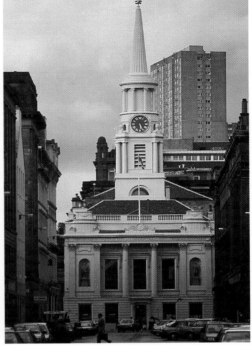

Hutchesons' Hall
Glasgow,
Strathclyde

Hutchesons' Hall.

The Tenement House
Glasgow,
Strathclyde

Piano and cat, The Tenement House.
The atmosphere in The Tenement House is
overwhelming, triggering off all kinds of
nostalgia. Sooty, the cat of the Trust's
representative, makes sure that, as the house
has not been lived in for a number of years,
no unwanted tenants survive there.

Goatfell
Isle of Arran,
Strathclyde

North-west ridge of Cir Mhór.

Rock forms, summit of Cir Mhór.

Ascending Cir Mhór.
I spent a day on the Arran hills with a group of Trust rangers. After having had a clear sunny start, we neared the top of Cir Mhór only to be enveloped in dense cloud.

Glacial deposits, Glen Rosa.

Resting party: view of Cir Mhór, Glen Rosa.
As we left the top of Cir Mhór the cloud began to open, and by the time we were resting down in Glen Rosa, it was virtually clear again.

Brodick Castle
Isle of Arran, Strathclyde

John Basford, Head Gardener, Brodick Castle Garden.
John is a delightful character and one could never guess that behind his modest facade lies a world authority on rhododendrons. His affinity with the Brodick gardens is no more apparent than when he is entertaining visitors on his regular summertime guided walks.

Formal border, Brodick Castle Garden.
'Oh, this year's colours are very ordinary, not half so good as last year's. We'll be getting them out shortly.' John Basford's reply to my admiring comments on some superb workmanship by his gardeners at Brodick.

Brodick Castle, west front.

Culzean Castle and Country Park
Kyle and Carrick, Strathclyde

Culzean Castle from cliff walk.

**Winkle-pickers on the beach below
Culzean Castle.**

Shoreline walk, Culzean Castle Country Park.

One of the great pleasures of Culzean is being in the vicinity of the Home Farm visitor centre when it is engulfed by children, enthusiastically waiting to go out and explore the surrounding environment. Under the guidance of the ranger team at Culzean they experience areas ranging from coastline, gardens, ponds, many miles of woodland walks to a newly created tree-top walk up amongst the squirrels. I came originally, like many visitors, to see the castle and its superb setting overhanging the sea; and then discovered the country park and its wealth of offerings.

**Bluebells, cliff walk, Culzean Castle
Country Park.**

Fountain Court, Culzean Castle.

Swan Pond, Culzean Castle Country Park.

Glenluce Abbey glebe
Wigtown,
Dumfries and Galloway

Glenluce Abbey glebe.
The Trust owns the glebe at Glenluce, which
is the area of ground surrounding the Abbey;
it is used as a farm field.

Rockcliffe beach looking towards Rough Island.

Although not owning the beach at Rockcliffe, the Trust does own and protect quite a few properties in this area, including Rough Island, which is a bird sanctuary. Access to Jubilee Path and Muckle Lands, the area of rough coastline between Rockcliffe and Kippford owned by the Trust, is gained at the far end of the beach.

Rockcliffe
Stewartry,
Dumfries and Galloway

Threave Garden
Castle Douglas, Stewartry,
Dumfries and Galloway

**Gardening school walkabout,
Threave Garden.**
Led by Bill Hean, principal of Threave School
of Gardening, the students go on a weekly
discussion walk around the grounds.

**Threave House and daffodil bank,
Threave Garden.**

**Ground cover, springtime,
Threave Garden.**

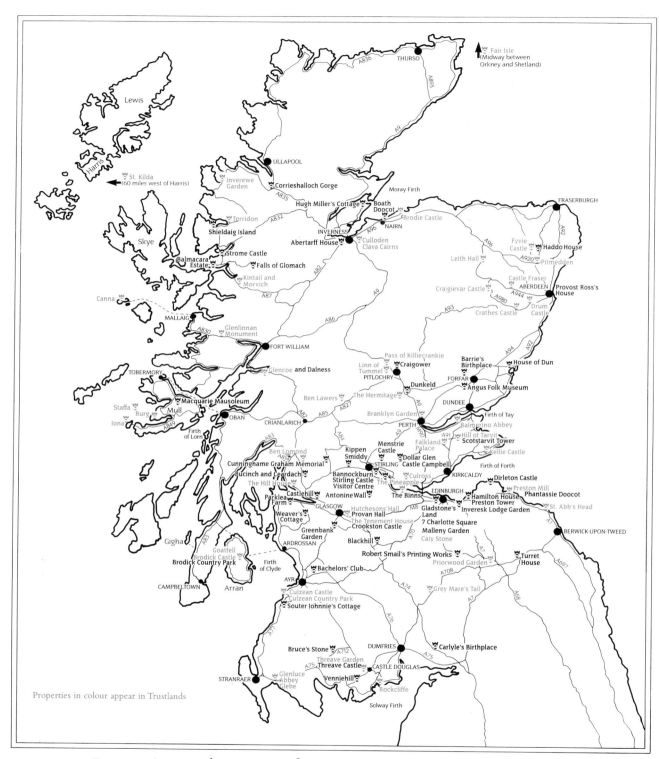

Properties in colour appear in Trustlands

Properties in the Care of ♛ National Trust for Scotland

INDEX